John Kember and Juliet Dammers

Cello Sight-Reading 2

Déchiffrage pour le violoncelle 2
Vom-Blatt-Spiel auf dem Cello 2

A fresh approach / Nouvelle approche
Eine erfrischend neue Methode

ED 12965
ISMN M-2201-2614-7
ISBN 978-1-84761-023-2

SCHOTT

www.schott-music.com

Mainz · London · Berlin · Madrid · New York · Paris · Prague · Tokyo · Toronto
© 2007 SCHOTT MUSIC Ltd, London · Printed in Germany

ED 12965

British Library Cataloguing-in-Publication Data.
A catalogue record for this book is available from the British Library
ISMN M-2201-2614-7
ISBN 978-1-84761-023-2

French translation: Agnès Ausseur
German translation: Ute Corleis
Cover design by www.adamhaystudio.com
Music setting and page layout by Bev Wilson
Printed in Germany S&Co.8276

Contents
Sommaire/Inhalt

Preface

Cello Sight-Reading 2 aims to build on the sight-reading skills learnt in book 1 and provide a wealth of more challenging examples so that the pupil may gain even greater confidence when approaching any new piece of music for the first time.

There are five sections which gradually introduce position changing, new time signatures, clefs, articulations, dynamics, double stops and Italian terms in a logical sequence, much as you would find in a cello tutor. The emphasis is on providing idiomatic tunes and structures rather than sterile sight-reading exercises.

Each section begins with several solo examples and concludes with duets and accompanied pieces, enabling the player to gain experience of sight-reading within the context of ensemble playing.

The player is urged to consider each piece initially for its rhythmic content, but with awareness of tempo and style. Students are encouraged to perform each piece in the manner of style indicated and to play not only fluently but also musically and expressively: an interesting and musically shaped performance is always preferable to one that is technically correct but dull.

Section 1 revises work covered in book 1 before introducing 4th position on the A string. More complex rhythms are used.

Section 2 encourages the use of 4th position on all four strings in preparation for more position work from Section 3 onwards.

Section 3 makes use of all positions up to 4th but begins with solos that stay in one position before introducing position changing. Fingerings are given to help in early examples but students are encouraged to think for themselves after that. The tenor clef is also introduced.

Section 4 requires a sound knowledge of position work and extends the range. Irregular time signatures and swing rhythms are introduced.

Section 5 introduces the treble clef and thumb position before extending the range still further and using more demanding keys.

To the pupil

The object of these pieces is to encourage the habit of sight-reading, both in solo form and in duets and accompanied pieces, in order to prepare you for reading in both solo and ensemble situations.

It is always recommended that your first consideration should be to realize the overall style of each piece and to establish a pulse in your mind before you begin to play. This can be achieved very quickly with practice.

Be constantly aware of the key and accidentals required in each piece and always look out for changes that may occur in both the accidentals and the time signatures. You are encouraged to look ahead and plan fingerings and changes of position.

Above all, aim to **play musically** by creating shape as indicated by the dynamics and phrasing. Call on your experience to give a stylistic, expressive and musical interpretation at all times.

Reading at sight is an essential 'life' skill for all musicians. It gives you the **independence** to explore **your choice** of music for yourself, drawing material from either the past or today's popular repertoire.

> **Always** be careful to observe time and key signatures.
> **Always** consider the rhythms first.
> **Always** aim to maintain continuity and pulse.
> And, above all, **always** attempt to play musically.

Be independent: be free to choose, explore and enjoy!

Fingerings

Although there are many different ways to finger certain passages, try to use any suggested fingerings as they are there to encourage you to play in particular positions and enable you to become confident in using them – particularly in Sections 2 and 3.

Préface

Déchiffrage pour le violoncelle 2 s'appuie sur les aptitudes de lecture à vue acquises dans le volume 1 et présente une multitude de configurations plus exigeantes qui renforceront l'assurance de l'élève lors de sa première approche d'une pièce de musique.

Les cinq parties de ce volume introduisent progressivement changements de position, mesures, clefs, phrasés, nuances, doubles cordes et termes italiens nouveaux selon un ordre logique respectant celui d'une méthode de violoncelle. Le propos est ici d'offrir des morceaux de musique et des structures caractéristiques de la musique pour violoncelle de préférence à de stériles exercices de déchiffrage.

Chaque partie débute par plusieurs pièces en solo et se termine par des duos et des pièces accompagnées qui familiariseront avec le déchiffrage dans le cadre de l'exécution collective.

Le lecteur est fortement incité à envisager en priorité le contenu rythmique de chaque pièce, tout en considérant le *tempo* et le style, et à interpréter chaque pièce dans le style indiqué avec aisance, musicalité et expression. Une interprétation construite et musicale sera toujours préférable à une exécution techniquement correcte mais sans relief.

1ère partie – Révision du travail effectué dans le premier volume puis introduction de la 4ème position sur la corde de *la*. Rythmes plus complexes.

2ème partie – Recours à la 4ème position sur les quatre cordes en préparation du travail sur les positions proposé à partir de la 3ème partie.

3ème partie – Toutes les positions jusqu'à la 4ème, en commençant par des solos gardant la même position avant d'introduire des changements de position. Les doigtés sont indiqués dans les premiers exemples, ensuite, l'interprète sera amené à établir son propre doigté. Introduction de la clef d'*ut* 4ème ligne.

4ème partie – Extension de la tessiture fondée sur une bonne connaissance du travail des positions. Introduction des mesures irrégulières et de la rythmique *swing*.

5ème partie – Introduction de la clef de *sol* et de la position du pouce avant une plus grande extension de la tessiture et le recours à des tonalités plus exigeantes.

A l'élève

Le propos de ces morceaux est d'encourager l'habitude du déchiffrage en solo, en duo ou accompagné au piano, de manière à préparer à la lecture à vue en soliste ou collective.

Il est recommandé de toujours envisager en premier lieu le style général de chaque pièce et d'établir une pulsation intérieure avant de commencer à jouer. Ceci s'acquiert très rapidement avec de l'entraînement.

Ayez constamment la tonalité de chaque pièce et les altérations qu'elle comporte présentes à l'esprit. Repérez les changements d'altérations et de mesure survenant en cours de morceau. Efforcez-vous de lire à l'avance et de prévoir doigtés et changements de position.

Avant tout, jouer **avec musicalité** en respectant le caractère défini par les nuances dynamiques et le phrasé. Appuyez-vous sur votre expérience pour donner à tout moment une interprétation stylée, expressive et musicale.

La lecture à vue est essentielle à la « survie » de tout musicien. Elle procure une **indépendance** permettant l'exploration par vous-même de la musique de **votre choix**, du répertoire passé ou contemporain.

> **Toujours** repérer les indications de mesure et de tonalité.
> **Toujours** envisager le rythme en premier lieu.
> **Toujours** s'efforcer de maintenir continuité et pulsation.
> **Toujours**, et surtout, jouer avec musicalité.

L'indépendance procure la liberté de choisir, d'explorer et de se faire plaisir !

Doigtés

Quoiqu'il existe plusieurs manières de doigter certains passages, obligez-vous à utiliser les doigtés proposés qui vous donneront plus d'assurance dans certaines positions, en particulier dans la 2ème et la 3ème parties.

Vorwort

Vom-Blatt-Spiel auf dem Cello 2 baut auf den Blatt-Spiel Fähigkeiten auf, die in Band 1 erworben wurden, und stellt eine Fundgrube mit anspruchsvolleren Beispielen dar, so dass der Schüler mit noch mehr Selbstvertrauen an die Erarbeitung eines neuen Musikstücks herangehen wird.

Es gibt fünf Teile, die nach und nach Lagenwechsel sowie neue Taktarten, Notenschlüssel, Artikulation, Dynamik, Doppelgriffe und italienische Begriffe in einer logischen Abfolge einführen. Also ganz ähnlich, wie es ein Cellolehrer auch machen würde. Der Schwerpunkt liegt auf idiomatischen Melodien und Strukturen statt sterilen Blatt-Spiel Übungen.

Jeder Teil beginnt mit mehreren Solobeispielen und endet mit Duetten und begleiteten Stücken. Dadurch kann der Spieler auch Erfahrungen im Blatt-Spiel beim gemeinsamen Musizieren mit anderen machen.

Auch in diesem Band wird der Leser dazu aufgefordert, jedes Stück erst einmal auf seinen rhythmischen Gehalt hin zu betrachten, aber mit dem zusätzlichen Bewusstsein für Tempo und Stil. Die Schüler werden dazu ermutigt, jedes Stück in der angegebenen Stilart wiederzugeben, und dabei nicht nur flüssig, sondern auch musikalisch und ausdrucksvoll zu spielen: eine interessante und musikalische Darbietung ist grundsätzlich einer technisch korrekten, aber langweiligen vorzuziehen.

Teil 1 wiederholt Dinge, die in Band 1 behandelt wurden, bevor die 4. Lage auf der A-Saite eingeführt wird. Außerdem werden komplexere Rhythmen benutzt.

Teil 2 ermutigt zur Benutzung der 4. Lage auf allen vier Saiten, was als Vorbereitung zu weiterer Lagenarbeit dient.

Teil 3 benutzt alle Lagen bis zur 4., beginnt aber mit Solostücken, die innerhalb einer Lage bleiben bevor Änderungen eingeführt werden. In den ersten Beispielen sind zur Hilfe Fingersätze angegeben, aber danach werden die Schüler dazu ermutigt, eigene zu überlegen. Der Tenorschlüssel wird eingeführt.

Teil 4 erfordert eine gründliche Kenntnis der Lagenarbeit und erweitert den Tonraum. Unregelmäßige Taktarten und Swingrhythmen werden vorgestellt.

Teil 5 führt den Violinschlüssel und die Daumenlage ein, bevor der Tonraum wieder erweitert wird und ungewohnte Tonarten benutzt werden.

An den Schüler

Ziel ist es, mit diesen Stücken die Gewohnheit des Vom-Blatt-Spiels weiter zu festigen. Das soll sowohl mit solistischen Stücken als auch mit Duetten und begleiteten Stücken geschehen. Dadurch wirst du darauf vorbereitet, sowohl in Solo- als auch in kammermusikalischen Situationen vom Blatt zu lesen.

Dein erstes Augenmerk sollte immer dem Erkennen des vorherrschenden Stils in jedem Stückes gelten sowie der Verankerung eines Pulsschlages in deinem Kopf. Erst dann beginne zu spielen. Mit ein bisschen Übung kann das sehr schnell erreicht werden.

Sei dir immer der Tonart und den Vorzeichen, die in jedem Stück gebraucht werden, bewusst. Halte immer Ausschau nach Veränderungen, die sowohl bei den Vorzeichen als auch bei den Taktarten vorkommen können. Du wirst dazu ermutigt, Fingersätze und Lagenwechsel im Voraus zu planen.

Dein oberstes Ziel sollte es immer sein, **musikalisch** zu **spielen**, indem du die Form herausarbeitest, die durch Dynamik und Phrasierung angezeigt wird. Greife auf deine Erfahrung zurück, um jederzeit eine stilistische, ausdrucksstarke und musikalische Interpretation darzubieten.

Vom-Blatt Spielen ist eine wesentliche ‚Lebens'-Fähigkeit für alle Musiker. Sie bietet dir die **Unabhängigkeit**, deine **Musikauswahl** selbst zu treffen, wobei entweder Material aus der Vergangenheit oder aus dem heutzutage beliebten Repertoire herangezogen wird.

> Bestimme **immer** sehr sorgfältig Takt- und Tonart.
> Bedenke **immer** zuerst den Rhythmus.
> Setze dir zum Ziel, **immer** die Kontinuität und den Pulsschlag beizubehalten.
> Und vor allem anderen: versuche **immer**, musikalisch zu spielen.

Sei unabhängig: fühle dich frei, zu wählen, auszuloten und zu genießen!

Fingersätze

Obwohl es fingersatztechnisch viele unterschiedliche Arten gibt bestimmte Passagen zu spielen, versuche immer die vorgeschlagenen Fingersätze zu benutzen, da sie dich dazu ermutigen sollen bestimmte Lagen zu verwenden und dich dadurch mit ihrem Gebrauch vertraut machen – besonders in den Teilen 2 und 3.

Section 1 – 4th position on the A string and the harmonic A
1ère partie – 4ème position sur la corde de *la* et son *la* harmonique
Teil 1 – Die 4. Lage auf der A-Saite und Flageolett-A

Reading at sight: giving a musical performance

1. Look at the **time signature** and check for any changes within the piece. Tap the rhythm, feeling the pulse throughout. Count at least one bar in your head before you begin to play.

2. Look at the **key signature**. Identify the notes that the sharps and flats apply to. Also look for **accidentals** in the piece.

3. Look for **fingerings** and **plan ahead for changes of position**.

4. Look for **patterns**. While tapping the rhythm, look at the melodic shape and notice movement by step and interval, repeated notes and sequences.

5. Observe the **articulations** and **dynamics**.

6. Above all, give a **musical performance** of each piece. Before you begin, observe the character of the music given in the performance directions. Look ahead while playing and keep going.

La lecture à vue est d'abord une exécution musicale

1. Vérifiez l'**indication de mesure** et recherchez les changements se produisant au cours de la pièce. Frappez le rythme en maintenant une pulsation intérieure constante. Comptez au moins une mesure mentalement avant de commencer à jouer.

2. Vérifiez l'**indication de la tonalité**. Repérez à quelles notes s'appliquent les altérations. Recherchez également les **altérations accidentelles**.

3. Repérez les **doigtés** et **prévoyez les changements de position**.

4. Repérez les **motifs**. Tout en frappant le rythme, observez les contours mélodiques et notez les déplacements par degré, les sauts d'intervalles, les notes répétées et les séquences.

5. Examiner les **phrasés** et les **nuances dynamiques**.

6. Avant tout, donnez une **interprétation musicale** de chaque morceau. Avant de commencer, cernez le caractère de la musique à l'aide des indications d'exécution, lisez à l'avance pendant que vous jouez et, surtout, ne vous arrêtez pas.

Vom Blatt lesen: eine musikalische Vorstellung geben

1. Schaue dir die **Taktart** genau an und überprüfe das ganze Stück auf eventuelle Taktartänderungen. Schlage den Rhythmus und fühle durchweg den Pulsschlag. Zähle mindestens einen Takt im Kopf vor, bevor du zu spielen beginnst.

2. Jetzt schaue auf die **Tonart**. Suche die Noten heraus, zu denen die Kreuz- und B-Vorzeichen gehören. Achte auch auf **Vorzeichen** innerhalb des Stückes.

3. Schaue dir die **Fingersätze** an und **plane die Lagenwechsel im Voraus**.

4. Achte auf **Muster**. Betrachte die melodische Form, während du den Rhythmus schlägst, und erkenne Schritt- und Sprungbewegungen sowie sich wiederholende Noten und Sequenzen.

5. Nun studiere **Artikulation** und **Dynamik**.

6. Am allerwichtigsten ist: mache aus jedem Stück eine **musikalische Darbietung**. Bevor du anfängst, schaue dir noch den Charakter der Musik, der sich in den Vortragsangaben widerspiegelt, genau an, schaue beim Spielen immer nach vorne und, vor allem, spiele immer weiter.

Glossary of terms new to this section:
Glossaire des termes nouveaux :
Vortragsangaben für Teil 1:

A tempo	return to original tempo	au mouvement original	im Takt
Allegro	quick, fast	rapide	schnell
Allegro moderato	moderately fast	modérément rapide	gemäßigt schnell
Allegretto	not as fast as allegro	moins rapide qu'*allegro*	weniger bewegt als Allegro
Andante	at a walking pace	allant	gehend
Andante moderato	at a moderate walking pace	modérément allant	in gemäßigtem Tempo
Andante e sentimentale	at a walking pace	allant et sentimental	mäßigt bewegt und sanft
Andante sostenuto	at a walking pace and sustained	allant et soutenu	verhalten
Ben marcato	well marked	bien marqué	markiert
Cantabile	in a singing style	chantant	gesanglich
Con moto	with movement	avec mouvement	mit Bewegung
Con spirito	with spirit	avec esprit	mit Geist
Deciso	decisive	décidé	bestimmt
Dolce	sweet	doux	süß
Espress., Espressivo	expressive	expressif	ausdrucksvoll
Giocoso	playful, humorous	joyeux	spielerisch, humorvoll
Largo	broad	large	breit
Maestoso	majestic	majestueusement	majestätisch
Misterioso	mysterious	mystérieux	geheimnisvoll
Moderato	moderate (at a moderate pace)	modéré	gemäßigt
Molto	much, very	très, beaucoup	sehr
Poco a poco	little by little	peu à peu	nach und nach
Poco lento	a little slowly	un peu lent	etwas langsamer
Poco rall. (rallentando)	gradually getting a little slower	en ralentissant	langsamer werdend
Poco rit. (ritenuto)	held back	retenu	zurückhaltend
Risoluto	with resolve	résolu	entschlossen
Ritmico	rhythmic	rythmé	rhythmisch
Scherzando	jokingly	en badinant	spielerisch, scherzend
Subito (sub.)	suddenly	soudain	plötzlich
Tempo di valzer	at the speed of a waltz	rythme de valse	im Walzertempo
⌢ (corona)	fermata (pause)	point d'orgue	Fermate

Section 1 – 4th position on the A string and the harmonic A

1ère partie – 4ème position sur la corde de *la* et son
la harmonique

Teil 1 – Die 4. Lage auf der A-Saite und Flageolett-A

10

4. **Con spirito**

5. **Andante**

6. **Andante sostenuto**

7. **Maestoso**

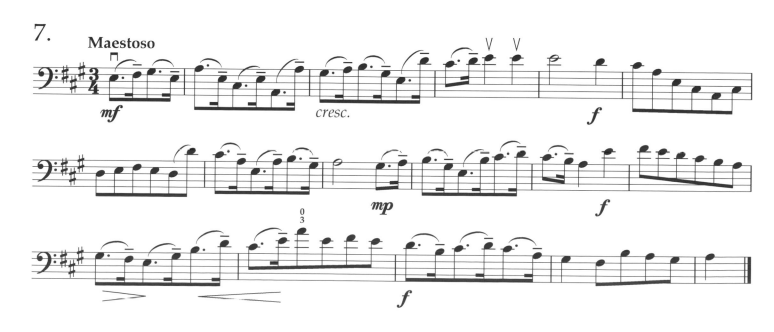

12

15.

Scherzando

16.

Ritmico

17.

Andante e sentimentale

18.
Maestoso

19.
Allegretto

22. Poco lento

23. Andante moderato

24.

25.

Giocoso

poco a poco dim.

26. Deciso

27.

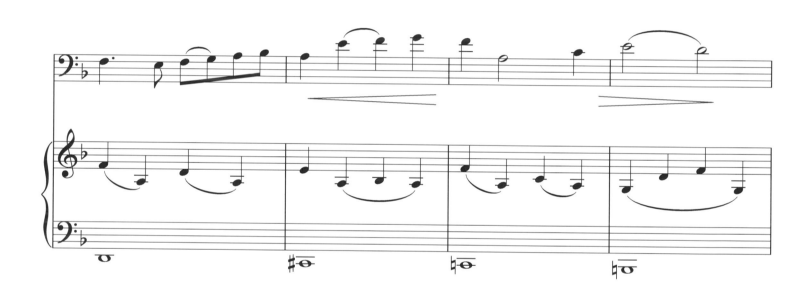

28.

Scherzando

Section 2 – 4th position on all strings
2ème partie – 4ème position sur toutes les cordes
Teil 2 – Die 4. Lage auf allen Saiten

Reading at sight: giving a musical performance

1. Identify the **character** of the piece – fast, slow, happy, march etc.

2. Observe the **time** and **key signatures** together with the **accidentals**, **dynamics**, **articulations**, **bow markings** and any other instructions. Look for **fingerings and plan ahead** for **changes of position**.

3. Choose an **appropriate speed**, both for the piece and for yourself – ensure that you are going to be comfortable enough to make a musical and technically accurate performance at the first attempt. Count at least one bar before you begin to play so as to secure the right speed.

4. While playing, always **look ahead** so that you have time to prepare for what is coming. In addition to playing the **right notes** with **rhythmic accuracy**, keep paying attention to all of the details as they occur: slurs, staccato, dynamics and any other instructions in the score.

5. Above all, give a **musical performance** of each piece. Before you begin, observe the character of the music as given in the performance directions; and keep going.

La lecture à vue est d'abord une exécution musicale

1. Cernez le **caractère** du morceau : rapide, lent, joyeux, marche, etc.

2. Observez les indications de **mesure** et de **tonalité**, ainsi que les **altérations accidentelles**, les **nuances**, le **phrasé**, les **coups d'archet** et toutes autres indications. Repérez les **doigtés** et prévoyez les **changements de position**.

3. Etablissez un **mouvement convenable** à la fois pour la pièce et pour vous-même. Assurez-vous d'être assez à l'aise pour donner une exécution musicale et techniquement exacte au premier essai. Comptez au moins une mesure avant de commencer à jouer de manière à prendre la bonne vitesse.

4. Pendant que vous jouez, lisez toujours **à l'avance** afin d'avoir le temps de vous préparer à ce qui vient. Tout en exécutant les **notes justes** avec **exactitude rythmique**, ne relâchez pas votre attention aux détails au fur et à mesure de leur apparition : liaisons, staccatos, nuances et autres indications portées sur la partition.

5. Avant tout, donnez une **interprétation musicale** de chaque morceau. Avant de commencer, cernez le caractère de la musique à l'aide des indications d'exécution, et, surtout, ne vous arrêtez pas.

Vom Blatt lesen: eine musikalische Vorstellung geben

1. Bestimme den **Charakter** des Stückes – schnell, langsam, fröhlich, marschartig, usw.

2. Beachte **Takt-** und **Tonart** sowie die **Vorzeichen**, **dynamische Angaben**, **Artikulationsbezeichnungen**, **Bogenstriche** und **sonstige Anweisungen**. Schaue dir die **Fingersätze** an und plane die **Lagenwechsel im Voraus**.

3. Wähle ein **geeignetes Tempo**, das sowohl dem Stück als auch deinem Können gerecht wird – versichere dich, dass du dich wohl genug fühlst, um gleich beim ersten Versuch eine musikalische und technisch genaue Vorstellung zu geben. Um das richtige Tempo zu verankern, zähle mindestens einen Takt im Kopf vor, bevor du zu spielen beginnst.

4. **Schaue** beim Spielen immer **voraus**, damit du genügend Zeit hast, um dich auf das Kommende vorzubereiten. Achte zusätzlich zum Spielen der **richtigen Noten** mit **rhythmischer Genauigkeit** auf alle **Details**, wenn sie auftauchen: Bindungen, Stakkato, Dynamik und alle anderen Anweisungen.

5. Am allerwichtigsten ist: mache aus jedem Stück eine **musikalische Darbietung**. Bevor du anfängst, schaue dir noch den Charakter der Musik, der sich in den Vortragsangaben widerspiegelt, genau an, und spiele immer weiter.

Glossary of terms new to this section:
Glossaire des termes nouveaux :
Neue Vortragsangaben in Teil 2:

Adagio	slow	lent	langsam
Alla giga	in the style of a gigue	en style de gigue	im Stile einer Gigue
Alla marcia	in the style of a march	en style de marche	im Stile eines Marsches
Allegro ma non troppo	fast, but not too fast	rapide mais pas trop	schnell, aber nicht zu schnell
Andantino	slightly faster than andante	un peu plus vite qu'*andante*	etwas schneller als Andante
Bossa nova	a dance from Brazil	bossa nova, danse brésilienne	brasilianischer Tanzstil
Doloroso	sadly	douloureux	schmerzlich
Hornpipe	a dance associated with	danse traditionnelle écossaise	traditioneller Tanz im
Grazioso	graceful	gracieux	anmutig
Larghetto	somewhat quicker and	plus court et plus rapide	kürzer und schneller als Largo
Leggiero	light	léger	leicht
Lento	slow	lent, large	langsam
Niente	nothing	rien	nichts
Presto	very fast	très vite	sehr schnell
Sostenuto	sustained	soutenu	zurückhaltend
Spiritoso	spirited	avec esprit	geistvoll
Tenuto (*ten.*)	held	tenu	gehalten
Tranquillo	tranquil, peaceful	calme	ruhig
Valse	waltz	valse	Walzer

Section 2 – 4th position on all strings
2ème partie – 4ème position sur toutes les cordes
Teil 2 – Die 4. Lage auf allen Saiten

Nos. 29–33 to be played in 4th position throughout.

Jouer les pièces n° 29 à 33 entièrement sur la 4ème position.

Die Stücke 29 bis 33 sollten in der 4. Lage gespielt werden.

Moving to and from 4th position.

Déplacement de et vers la 4ème position.

Lagenwechsel von der 1. in die 4. Lage und zurück.

44.

Andante

Both parts to be played in
4th position throughout.

Jouer les deux parties
entièrementsur la 4ème position.

Beide Stimmen sollten in
der 4. Lage gespielt werden.

45.

Larghetto

Changing position.   Changement de position.   Lagenwechsel.

46. Adagio

47. Allegretto

48.

50.

Alla marcia

51.

53.

54.

55.

Tranquillo

56.

Bossa nova

57. Valse

Section 3 – All positions up to 4th and the tenor clef
3ème partie – Toutes les positions jusqu'à la 4ème position et clef d'*ut* 4ème ligne
Teil 3 – Alle Lagen bis zur 4. und der Tenorschlüssel

Reading at sight: giving a musical performance

1. Identify the **character** of the piece and choose an appropriate tempo.

2. Check the **clef** at the start and look for any changes during the piece. Look at the **key signature** and any **accidentals**.

3. Look for **fingerings and plan ahead** for **changes of position**. Try to follow these fingerings carefully.

4. Observe the **bow markings**, **articulations** and **dynamics**.

5. Aim to give a **musical performance** of each piece. Before you begin, observe the character of the music as indicated in the performance directions. Look ahead while you are playing and keep going.

Modes
At the time of the ancient Greeks, musical notes were arranged into modes, and each mode has its own distinct sound and character. Over the centuries the modes changed and developed, and eventually two of them – the Ionian and the Aeolian – became what we now know as the major and minor scales. We can still hear modes in music that is performed today, such as in plainsong (the music of the medieval Church) and in the folk music of many countries. Today, jazz musicians play and improvise using all seven modes.
The most familiar mode is the Dorian mode (number 83) which uses the scale from D – D with the piano white notes only.

La lecture à vue est d'abord une exécution musicale

1. Cernez le caractère de la musique et choisissez un *tempo* convenable.

2. Vérifiez la **clef** en début de pièce et notez les changements de clef en cours de morceau. Assurez-vous de l'**armure** de la tonalité et repérez les **altérations accidentelles**.

3. Repérez les **doigtés** et prévoyez les **changements de position**. Efforcez-vous de respecter scrupuleusement les doigtés.

4. Observez les indications de **coups d'archet**, de **phrasé** et de **nuances**.

5. Donnez une **interprétation musicale** de chaque morceau. Avant de commencer, cernez le caractère de la musique à l'aide des indications d'exécution, lisez à l'avance pendant que vous jouez et, surtout, ne vous arrêtez pas.

Modes
Du temps de l'antiquité grecque, les notes étaient ordonnées selon des modes qui possédaient leur sonorité et leur caractère propres. Au cours des siècles, les modes se sont modifiés et ont évolué jusqu'à ce que deux d'entre eux – le mode ionien et le mode éolien – nous soient connus comme le mode majeur et le mode mineur. Les modes sont toujours utilisés dans quelques types de musiques comme le plain-chant et la musique traditionnelle de certaines régions. Les musiciens de jazz actuels jouent et improvisent dans les sept modes.
Le mode le plus couramment usité est le mode dorien (n°83) formé sur une échelle allant de *ré* à *ré* sans altération.

Vom Blatt lesen: eine musikalische Vorstellung geben

1. Bestimme den **Charakter** des Stückes und wähle ein geeignetes Tempo.

2. Schaue dir den **Notenschlüssel** am Anfang an und suche alle Änderungen innerhalb des Stückes. Beachte die **Taktart** und alle zusätzlichen **Vorzeichen**.

3. Schaue dir die **Fingersätze** an und **plane die Lagenwechsel im Voraus**. Halte diese Fingersätze sorgfältig ein.

4. Achte auf **Bogenstriche**, **Artikulation** und **Dynamik**.

5. Am allerwichtigsten ist: mache aus jedem Stück eine **musikalische Darbietung**. Bevor du anfängst, schaue dir noch den Charakter der Musik, der sich in den Vortragsangaben widerspiegelt, genau an, schaue beim Spielen immer nach vorne und, vor allem, spiele immer weiter.

Kirchentonarten
Zur Zeit der alten Griechen wurden die Musiknoten zu Tonarten, den späteren Kirchentonarten, zusammengestellt, von denen jede ihren ganz eigenen Klang und Charakter hat. Über die Jahrhunderte hinweg veränderten und entwickelten sich diese Kirchentonarten. Schließlich wurden zwei von ihnen, Ionisch und Äolisch, das, was heutzutage als Dur- und Moll-Tonleiter bekannt ist. Wir können auch heute noch Kirchentonarten in aufgeführter Musik hören, z.B. im gregorianischen Gesang (der Musik der mittelalterlichen Kirche) und in der Volksmusik vieler Länder. Heutzutage spielen und improvisieren Jazzmusiker in allen sieben Kirchentonarten.
Die bekannteste Kirchentonart ist dorisch (Nummer 83), die die Tonleiter von D – D benutzt. Auf dem Klavier werden dabei nur die weißen Tasten gespielt.

Glossary of terms new to this section:
Glossaire des termes nouveaux :
Weitere Vortragsangaben:

Allargando	broadening out	en élargissant	breiter werdend
Allegro con spirito	fast, with spirit	rapide, avec esprit	geistreich
Andante cantabile	at a walking pace and in a singing style	allant et chantant	gehend und gesangvoll
Con brio	with vigour	enlevé	schwungvoll
Semplice	simple	simplement	einfach
Sempre	always	toujours	immer/stets
Scherzo	joke	badinerie	Scherz
Vivo	lively	vif	lebhaft

Section 3 – All positions up to 4th and the tenor clef
3ème partie – Toutes les positions jusqu'à la 4ème position et clef d'*ut* 4ème ligne
Teil 3 – Alle Lagen bis zur 4. und der Tenorschlüssel

Stay in the same position throughout.   Garder la même position jusqu'au bout.   Bleibe in der gleichen Lage.

Stay in the same position throughout.   Garder la même position jusqu'au bout.   Bleibe in der gleichen Lage.

Changing position.   Changement de position.   Lagenwechsel.

The tenor clef.   Clef d'*ut* 4ème ligne.   Tenorschlüssel.

71.

Allegro con spirito

Sempre pizz.

72.

Sostenuto

73.

Andante cantabile

46

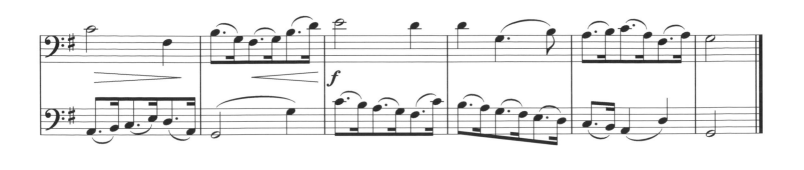

76.

Con brio

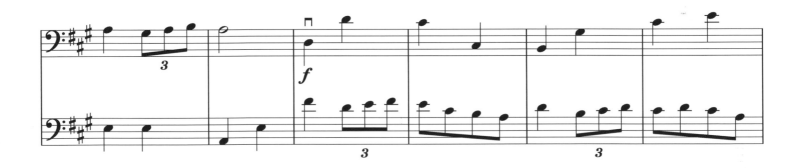

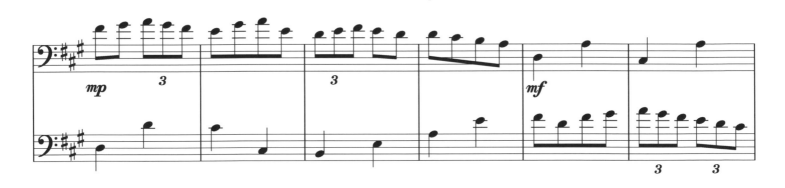

poco rit.

48

77.

Spiritoso

78.

79.

81

Con moto

mf

rit.

a tempo

52

83.

Section 4 – Irregular time signatures and swing
4ème partie – Mesures irrégulières et rythmique *swing*
Teil 4 – Unregelmäßige Taktarten und Swing

Reading at sight: giving a musical performance

1. Identify the **character** of the piece and choose an **appropriate tempo**.

2. Check the **clef** at the start and look for any changes during the piece. Look at the **key signature** and any **accidentals**.

3. Look through and **plan fingerings** – try to stay in the same position wherever you can.

4. Observe the **articulations** and **dynamics**.

5. Above all, give a **musical performance** of each piece. Before you begin, observe the performance directions; keep looking ahead while you are playing and keep going.

Swing rhythms
Swing rhythms are what most people think of as 'jazz', with their easily recognisable, relaxed triplet feel. There are many forms of jazz: Dixieland, blues, traditional, swing, bebop and many others. Common to most is a flexible notation of rhythm born out of the fact that jazz is mostly an aural tradition. Interpreting 'jazz quavers' (eighth notes) is the main rhythmic focus of this section.

Jazz quavers can be notated in two ways:

or

both played:

La lecture à vue est d'abord une exécution musicale

1. Cernez le caractère de la musique et choisissez un *tempo* convenable.

2. Vérifiez la **clef** en début de pièce et notez les changements de clef en cours de morceau. Assurez-vous de l'**armure** de la tonalité et repérez les **altérations accidentelles**.

3. Parcourez la pièce et **prévoyez les doigtés** – Efforcez-vous de maintenir, si possible, la même position.

4. Examiner les **phrasés** et les **nuances dynamiques**.

5. Avant tout, donnez une **interprét-ation musicale** de chaque morceau. Avant de commencer, observez les indications d'exécution, lisez à l'avance pendant que vous jouez et, surtout, ne vous arrêtez pas.

Rythmes *swing*
La rythmique swing, facilement reconnaissable à son allure ternaire libre, est généralement associée au jazz. Il existe diverses formes de jazz qui ont généralement en commun une notation rythmique souple issue du fait que le jazz est essentiellement une tradition orale.

Cette partie se concentre principalement sur l'interprétation des croches « jazz » qui peuvent être notées de deux façons :

ou

toutes deux exécutées :

Vom Blatt lesen: eine musikalische Vorstellung geben

1. Bestimme den **Charakter** des Stückes und wähle ein **geeignetes Tempo**.

2. Schaue dir den **Notenschlüssel** am Anfang an und suche alle Änderungen innerhalb des Stückes. Beachte die **Taktart** und alle zusätzlichen **Vorzeichen**.

3. Schaue dir das Stück an und **plane** deine **Fingersätze** im Voraus – versuche, falls möglich, in der selben Lage zu bleiben.

4. Achte auf **Artikulation** und **Dynamik**.

5. Am allerwichtigsten ist: mache aus jedem Stück eine **musikalische Darbietung**. Bevor du anfängst, mache dir mit den Vortragsanga-ben vertraut, schaue beim Spielen immer nach vorne und, vor allem, spiele immer weiter.

Swingrhythmen
Swingrhythmus ist das, was die meisten Leute unter ‚Jazz' verstehen, mit seinem leicht wiederzuerkennenden, entspannten Triolengefühl. Es gibt viele Formen des Jazz: Dixieland, Blues, Swing, Bebop und viele andere. Allen gemeinsame ist die flexible Rhythmusnotation, die dem Umstand entsprang, dass Jazz hauptsächlich eine über das Gehör überlieferte Tradition ist. Die Interpretation von ‚Jazz-Achteln' ist der Haupschwerpunkt dieses Teils.

Jazzachtel kann man auf zwei Arten notieren:

oder

Beide werden wie folgt gespielt:

Glossary of terms:
Glossaire des termes nouveaux :
Weitere Vortragsangaben:

Adagio maestoso	slow and majestic	lent et majesteux	langsam und majestätisch
Al valzer	in the style of a waltz	en style de valse	im Stile eines Walzers
Grandioso	in a grand manner	grandiose, noble	grandios, großartig
Grave	serious	sérieux	langsam und ernst
Marcato (*marc.*)	marked	marqué	markiert
Mesto	sad	triste	traurig
Passacaglia	a piece built over a repeated bass line	passacaille (pièce construite sur une basse obstinée)	ursprünglich ein spanischer Volkstanz, wobei ein Thema über einer sich wiederholenden Bassline variiert
Pesante	heavy	lourd	schwer, schwerfällig
Poco lento e ritmico	a little slowly and rhythmically	un peu lent et rythmé	etwas langsamer und rhythmisch
Ragtime	a syncopated early jazz style	style de jazz syncopé	ein früher Jazzstil mit synkopierter Melodie
Ritenuto	held back	retenu	zurückhaltend
Seconda volta	second time	deuxième fois	zum zweiten Mal
Tempo comodo	at a convenient speed	au mouvement convenable	gemächliches Tempo

Section 4 – Irregular time signatures and swing
4ème partie – Mesures irrégulières et rythmique *swing*

Teil 4 – Unregelmäßige Taktarten und Swing

100.

Andante moderato

101.

Moderato

102.

Adagio maestoso – passacaglia

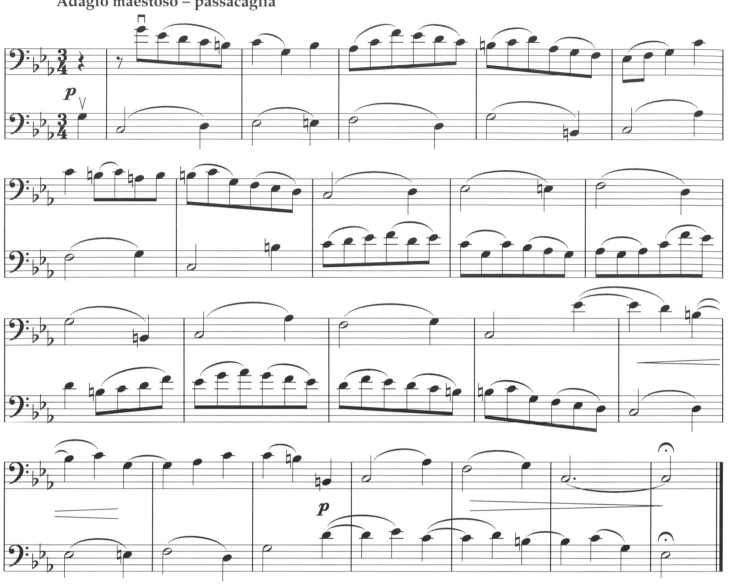

103.

Larghetto

104.

Poco lento e ritmico

105.

Grave

106.

107.

Ragtime

108.

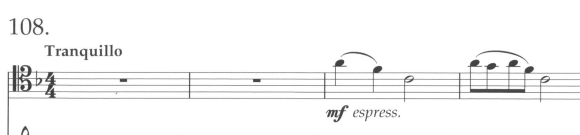

109.

110.

Section 5 – Thumb position and treble clef
5ème partie – Position du pouce et clef de *sol*
Teil 5 – Die Daumenlage und der Violinschlüssel

Reading at sight: giving a musical performance

1. Identify the **character** of the piece and choose an **appropriate tempo**.

2. Check the **clef** – bass, tenor or treble – and look for any changes during the piece. Look at the key signature and for any additional accidentals.

3. The first five solos in this section should be played entirely in the **thumb position**. Always look through and plan fingerings and try to stay in the same position as much as possible. Be ready for the high notes – hear them in your head before you move to them.

4. Observe **bowings**, **articulations** and **dynamics**.

5. Above all, give a **musical performance** of each piece. Before you begin, observe the performance directions; keep looking ahead and keep going.

Whole tone scale
The whole tone scale is made up entirely of notes a whole tone apart. There are only two:

Number 123 is an example of this style.

La lecture à vue est d'abord une exécution musicale

1. Cernez le caractère de la musique et choisissez un *tempo* convenable.

2. Vérifiez la **clef** – clef de *fa*, d'*ut* 4ème ligne ou de *sol* – et repérez tout changement de clef en cours de morceau, ainsi que l'armure de la tonalité et les altérations accidentelles.

3. Les cinq premiers solos de cette partie seront joués entièrement sur la **position du pouce**. Parcourez toujours la pièce avant de la jouer et prévoyez les doigtés. Obligez-vous à maintenir le plus possible la même position. Préparez-vous à jouer les notes aiguës – efforcez-vous de les entendre mentalement avant de vous déplacer vers elles.

4. Observez les indications de **coups d'archet**, de **phrasé** et de **nuances**.

5. Donnez, surtout, une **interprétation musicale** de chaque pièce. Avant d'attaquer, observez les indications de nuances. Lisez toujours à l'avance pendant que vous jouez et, surtout, ne vous arrêtez pas.

Gamme par tons entiers
La gamme par tons entiers est formée exclusivement de notes espacées d'un ton. Il n'en existe que deux :

La pièce n° 123 donne un exemple de la gamme par tons.

Vom Blatt lesen: eine musikalische Vorstellung geben

1. Bestimme den **Charakter** des Stückes und wähle ein **geeignetes Tempo**.

2. Schaue dir den **Notenschlüssel** an – Bass-, Tenor- oder Violinschlüssel – und suche alle Änderungen innerhalb des Stückes. Beachte die Taktart und alle zusätzlichen Vorzeichen.

3. Die ersten fünf Solostücke in diesem Teil sollten komplett in der **Daumenlage** gespielt werden. Schaue das Stück zuerst durch, plane die Fingersätze und versuche, solange wie möglich in der gleichen Lage zu bleiben. Sei auf die hohen Noten gefasst – höre sie in deinem Kopf, bevor du sie greifst.

4. Achte auf **Bogenstriche**, **Artikulation** und **Dynamik**.

5. Am allerwichtigsten ist: mache aus jedem Stück eine **musikalische Darbietung**. Bevor du anfängst, mache dich mit den Vortragsangaben vertraut, schaue beim Spielen immer nach vorne und, vor allem, spiele immer weiter.

Die Ganztonleiter
Eine Ganztonleiter besteht ausschließlich aus Noten, die einen Ganzton voneinander entfernt stehen. Davon gibt es nur zwei:

Stück Nr. 123 ist ein Beispiel für diesen Stil.

Atonal music

This is music without a sense of key although one note may act like a tonic. The music will sometimes have all twelve semitones set in a pre-determined order (known as a 'tone row') and will consequently contain a number of accidentals. Despite what may appear to be strange intervals, it is often music of great expression and therefore expression marks are of utmost importance. Composers such as Schoenberg, Webern and Berg were instrumental in the development of this style. Number 124 is an example of this idiom.

The double sharp

A single sharp raises the note by **one** semitone. A **double** sharp raises the note by **two** semitones.

The double sharp is notated:

Numbers 120 and 136 use the double sharp.

The double flat

A **single** flat lowers the note by **one** semitone. A **double** flat lowers the note by **two** semitones.

The double flat is notated:

Number 132 makes use of the double flat.

Musique atonale

Cette musique n'est pas régie par la tonalité quoiqu'une note puisse y avoir une fonction de tonique. Elle peut être construite sur un enchaînement des douze demi-tons placés dans un certain ordre (la « série ») et présentera donc un certain nombre d'altérations. Malgré certains intervalles qui déroutent, cette musique est souvent très expressive, les nuances y sont donc d'une importance essentielle. Les compositeurs Schoenberg, Webern et Berg furent les maîtres du développement de ce langage musical dont la pièce n° 124 fournit un exemplaire.

Le double dièse

Le **dièse** élève la note d'un demi-ton. Le **double dièse** élève la note de **deux** demi-tons.

Le double dièse est noté :

Les pièces nᵒˢ 120 et 136 recourent au double dièse.

Le double bémol

Le **bémol** abaisse la note d'un demi-ton. Le **double bémol** abaisse la note de **deux** demi-tons.

Le double bémol est noté :

La pièce n° 132 recourt au double bémol.

Atonale Musik

Das ist Musik ohne ein Tonartgefühl, obwohl eine Note wie eine Tonika agieren mag. Diese Musik beinhaltet manchmal alle zwölf Halbtöne in einer festgelegten Reihenfolge (der sogenannten ‚Zwölftonreihe') und wird demzufolge auch eine ganze Anzahl von Vorzeichen haben. Trotz der manchmal seltsam anmutenden Intervalle besitzt diese Musik oft große Ausdruckskraft. Daher sind auch die Ausdruckszeichen von allergrößter Wichtigkeit. Komponisten wie Schönberg, Webern und Berg waren bei der Entwicklung dieses Stils richtungweisend. Das Musikstück Nr. 124 ist ein Beispiel für dieses Idiom.

Das Doppelkreuz

Ein einfaches Kreuz erhöht die Note um **einen** Halbton. Ein **Doppelkreuz** erhöht die Note um **zwei** Halbtöne.

Das Doppelkreuz wird folgendermaßen notiert:

In den Stücken Nr. 120 und 136 kommen Doppelkreuze vor.

Das Doppel-b

Ein **einfaches** b erniedrigt die Note um **einen** Halbton. Ein **Doppel-b** erniedrigt die Note um **zwei** Halbtöne.

Das Doppel-b wird folgendermaßen notiert:

Im Stück Nr. 132 kommt das Doppel-b vor.

Glossary of terms new to this section:
Glossaire des termes nouveaux :
Weitere Vortragsangaben:

Lullaby (ninna nanna)	lullaby / cradle song	berceuse	Wiegenlied
Rubato	giving some flexibility in tempo	mouvement souple	geraubt, ein wenig frei
Sonore	with a resonant tone	sonore	klangvoll
Stringendo	gradually getting quicker	en resserrant progressivement	allmäßlich schneller werdend
Tempo ad lib.	freely – at your own tempo	tempo au choix de l'interprète	frei wählbares Tempo

Section 5 – Thumb position and treble clef
5ème partie – Position du pouce et clef de *sol*
Teil 5 – Die Daumenlage und der Violinschlüssel

Thumb position. Position du ponce. Daumenlage.

111.

112.

113.

All positions.   Toutes les positions.   Verschiedene Lagen.

116.

Lento

mp *sonore*

117.

Con moto

pizz. *sempre*

mp *leggiero*

cresc.

mp   *pp*   *sf*

74

121.

Allegretto con rubato

122.

Tempo ad lib.

Whole tone.   Gamme par tons.   Auf eine Ganztonleiter
                                                                          aufbauend.

123.

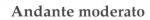

Tone row.   Série dodécaphonique.   Zwölftonreihe.

124.

125.

126.

127.

130.

131.

132.

133.

134.

135.

136.

137.

Glossary
Glossaire
Glossar

Note performance directions together with their translations used throughout the book so that you have a complete list. Writing them down will help you to remember them.

Inscrivez ici les indications d'exécution utilisées dans ce volume et leur traduction pour en établir une liste complète. Le fait de les noter vous aidera à les retenir.

Schreibe hier alle Vortragszeichen, die in diesem Band verwendet werden, zusammen mit ihrer Übersetzung auf, so dass du eine vollständige Liste hast. Das Aufschreiben wird dir dabei helfen, sie dir einzuprägen.

Adagio	Slowly	Lent	Langsam

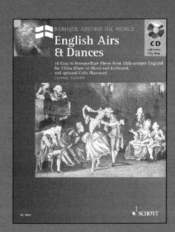
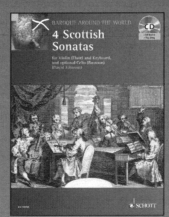

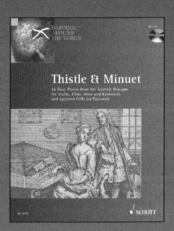